THE Four Corners
TIMELESS LANDS *of the* SOUTHWEST

by KATHLEEN BRYANT

MOAB

UTAH

COLORADO

89

BLANDING

CORTEZ

DURANGO

BLUFF

163

UTE
RESERVATION

SO. UTE RESERVATION

Lake Powell

Four
Corners

PAGE

160

SHIPROCK

AZTEC

TAOS

NAVAJO
RESERVATION

KAYENTA

FARMINGTON

191

Grand Canyon

ARIZONA

CHINLE

666

44

TUBA
CITY

Canyon
de Chelly

371

NEW MEXICO

GRAND
CANYON

HOPI
RESERVATION

89

WINDOW
ROCK

GALLUP

SANTA FE

FLAGSTAFF

SANDERS

GRANTS

ALBUQUERQUE

40

WINSLOW

ZUNI
RESERVATION

40

HOLBROOK

CONTENTS

Introduction 1

The People 3
    Navajo 5
    Hopi 19

The Lands 27
    Arizona 29
    New Mexico 39
    Colorado 47
    Utah 53

Resources 61

INTRODUCTION

Here on this dry, windswept plain, the sound of laughter mixes with the clicks and whirs of cameras as a young girl and her brother pose in a tangle of arms and legs. Beneath their hands and feet, a bronze marker placed by the U.S. Geological Survey bears the motto, "Four states here meet in freedom under God," a circular inscription that can be read from any of the four states of Arizona, New Mexico, Colorado, or Utah.

But the four corners are more than imaginary lines crossing the landscape. This spot marks the heart of the Southwest, where Navajo, Hopi, Zuni, and Ute people still carry on traditions begun by their ancestors hundreds, and even thousands, of years ago. When Spaniards and Americans arrived, native cultures accommodated new traditions without losing their own. The result is a complex tapestry of ceremony, art, cuisine, and custom, all woven on a loom of land and sky.

Far above the Four Corners monument, a raven inscribes his own circle in the sky. If he could fly high enough, he would see the four tall peaks that mark the boundaries of Navajo land, the sacred mountain of the Ute, and the canyons and mesas that ancestral Puebloans once called home. Land and culture are inseparable. At Wupatki, a large spiral petroglyph symbolizes the ancestors' journey. North of Flagstaff, the extinct volcano that forms the San Francisco Peaks is the summer home of the kachinas. And Monument Valley is a battle-field where spires and buttes mark the bodies of slain monsters.

From Holbrook, Arizona, to Cortez, Colorado, summer evenings echo with drumbeat and song as children perform dances they learned from their grandparents. Historic trading posts and contemporary galleries display native arts, from dazzling Navajo rugs to delicately carved Zuni fetishes. Juniper smoke, parched corn, and sizzling fry bread scent the air on festival days. Along scenic byways and winding mountain roads, parks and monuments preserve the ancient stone cities and offer sublime views of pine forests, slickrock canyons, and snow-capped mountains.

"My words are tied in one with the great mountains, with the great rocks, with the great trees," some Pueblo people sing, "in one with my body and my heart." Whether you begin in Cortez or Moab, Flagstaff or Gallup, you are about to journey into the very soul of the Southwest. May you travel in beauty.

the *People*

Though Four Corners country is lightly populated, it is rich with cultural tradition. Indian, Spanish, and Anglo influences blend into an intriguing mixture of language, story, food, and art. Casual western towns offer a relaxed atmosphere, along with the sights and sounds of feast days, festivals, and tribal fairs.

Tribal lands in particular give visitors the opportunity to step back in time. You can view prehistoric ruins or centuries-old pueblos and missions, as well as partake in cultural legacies that stretch back thousands of years. Through arts and crafts, the Southwest's native peoples have been able to carry their traditions into the modern world, as well as bolster tribal economies. In general, Indian nations depend on tourism and welcome visitors. However, as their guests, it is up to us to behave with courtesy and respect.

Reservations and pueblos are sovereign nations whose customs and tribal laws differ from ours. For example, alcoholic beverages and weapons are strictly prohibited. Many pueblo villages close completely during certain ceremonies. At the Hopi Mesas, social dances are often open to the public, but kachina ceremonies are rarely so. Practices vary among villages, so always check before attending. If you do attend, dress appropriately and observe respectfully.

Like our own cities and towns, reservation communities are places of residence and work, as well as worship. Check with visitor centers for tribal rules, especially those regarding photography. Many pueblos require permits and fees to carry cameras. Even so, photos of special places such as kivas, mission interiors, or cemeteries may be forbidden. Sketching and videotaping are also restricted. Never take photographs during a ceremony, and always ask an individual before taking his or her photo.

When traveling on native lands, stay on designated trails and roads and do not disturb or remove artifacts, rocks, plants, or animals. Be mindful that many locations throughout the Four Corners, such as Ship Rock, are considered sacred. Such places as Canyon de Chelly or Walpi village can be visited with a guide, an excellent opportunity to spend time with someone knowledgeable about area history.

Finally, always remember to travel with an open mind and a light heart. If you do, your journey will be memorable. As a Navajo chant says: "I have gone to the end of the earth. I have gone to the end of the waters. I have gone to the end of the sky. I have gone to the end of the mountains. I have found no one who was not my friend."

Left: Hoop dancers combine athleticism, grace, and precise timing to create intricate forms inspired by nature, such as a soaring eagle. *Above:* Navajo man.

Navajo
the Diné

Left: Desert varnish streaks the cliff above White House ruin in Canyon de Chelly. *Above:* A Navajo couple wears heishe-and-nugget, or "medicine man," necklaces. The loops of turquoise were once used as a form of currency. *Right:* Corn is an important element of Navajo life. *Pages 6-7:* According to legend, the Dancing Rocks near the town of Round Rock were once a man and woman, now turned to stone.

ROM THE POWERFUL SPIRES AND buttes of Monument Valley to the sweeping sandstone walls of Canyon de Chelly, Navajo Country is the classic southwestern landscape. The Navajo Reservation, the largest in the U.S., sprawls twenty-five thousand square miles across northeastern Arizona, western New Mexico, and into Utah. Movies, commercials, and landscape photographs all celebrate its quiet yet dramatic beauty. But the Navajo feel the land's beauty in their souls, saying, "With beauty all around me, I walk. With beauty within me, I walk."

As many as eleven thousand years ago, Athabaskan speakers migrated from Asia to North America. Some, who called themselves the Diné (the People), ventured further south about a thousand years ago, settling in a canyon near the headwaters of the San Juan River. They called their new homeland Dinétah. The earliest Navajo-style dwelling in Dinétah has been dated to the 1500s.

Nearby, the Diné encountered Pueblo dwellers whose settled lifestyle included corn agriculture. As the Diné adapted to their new homeland, they too incorporated corn into their repertoire of survival. During this time, life for the Diné was relatively peaceful. But for all southwestern tribes, this was the eve of change.

In 1540, Spanish explorer Francisco Vásquez de Coronado entered the Southwest, searching for the fabled seven golden cities of Cibola. He found only stone and adobe pueblos. Coronado left without the riches he sought but reported that colonization might be profitable.

Thus, in 1598, Don Juan de Oñate arrived with farmers, priests, servants, and an army escort, trailed by oxcarts and thousands of cattle, sheep, and goats. The colonists introduced the Southwest to peaches, metalwork, and horses. They gave, but they also took away.

New Spain's mines and ranches spurred an extensive slave trade, especially among the Navajo, whose semi-settled lifestyle made them difficult to convert and control. Fierce raiding and shifting alliances ensued between colonists, Navajo, Pueblo, Ute, and Comanche. The Pueblos revolted in 1680, driving out the Spanish. During the reconquest that followed, many Puebloans found refuge with the Navajo, intermarrying, exchanging lifeways (including weaving), and jointly defending themselves against Ute and Comanche raiders.

Conflict continued through Spanish, Mexican, and American rule, when the U.S. Army appointed famed scout Kit Carson to defend the territory. Carson's campaign against the Navajo focused on destroying herds, fields, and orchards. Within a matter of months, in January 1864, the Navajo agreed to go to Fort Sumner, New Mexico, also known as Bosque Redondo, land traditionally claimed by the Comanche.

The hardships of the campaign and the grueling four-hundred-mile winter march to Bosque Redondo are called the Long Walk. Those who didn't die or escape suffered four years of poor food, alkaline water, smallpox, Comanche raids, and crop-destroying hail and floods. The relocation was a nightmare, and the U.S. government knew it.

Navajo leaders argued eloquently for returning to their homeland. One leader said, "I think the world, the earth, and in the heavens we are all equal and we have all been born by the same mother—what we want is to be sent back to our own country."

In 1868, the Navajo returned home. In exchange for agreeing to stop raiding, the Navajo received rations, and later, sheep and goats. Herding became the foundation of the Navajo economy, and traders were awarded contracts to supply goods.

By the turn of the century, thirty-six traders lived on the reservation. Though some were

unscrupulous, many became trusted friends of the Navajo. Thomas Keams, J. B. Moore, and others often acted as representatives to the outside world, passing along news and explaining federal policies. "The role of the Navajo trader in the lives of the Indians was, most of the time, fundamental," the late Senator Barry Goldwater explained. "Whether providing white-man's medicine or an understanding ear, he tended to be there when needed."

Harry Goulding and his wife "Mike" began trading in 1924 from a tent on the border between Arizona and Utah, an area known as the Paiute Strip. They formed a strong bond with the local Navajo and built a permanent

Top left: Christopher "Kit" Carson.
Top right: This scene from Tuba City Trading Post in the early 1930s shows a rug with a whirling cross motif. The swastika is an ancient Vedic symbol for the sun. To other cultures, including the Navajo, the symbol can represent the four directions or the wind. Though once considered auspicious, the swastika came to be associated with destruction. Not surprisingly, rugs incorporating this motif dropped out of favor after World War II.
Above: Many trading posts offer "old pawn," or jewelry made in previous decades.
Left: Herders tend their flock below the silhouettes of Yei Bi Chai and Totem Pole in Monument Valley.

trading post in 1928, which still stands today. Shortly after the Gouldings established their permanence in the region, the U.S. government ordered stock reductions to combat overgrazing on the reservation, and the Monument Valley Navajo were especially hard hit. Using their resources, the Gouldings looked for ways to bolster the local economy and found the solution in Hollywood.

The movie industry helped ease the Depression, but World War II brought even greater changes. Thousands of young Navajos entered the war. Many trained for a special duty, as Code Talkers. The complex Navajo language was used as a double code—and it was never broken.

When soldiers returned to Navajo Country, jobs were scarce. With better roads, many chose to drive to larger off-reservation towns such as Gallup and Flagstaff to do their shopping or to find work. These and other changes spelled a slow decline for the trading post economy.

Today, a few posts still exist in the form of convenience stores. Others, geared to travelers, continue to promote traditional crafts. Hubbell Trading Post National Historic Site in Ganado, Arizona is a living example of how a classic trading post looked and operated.

In John Lorenzo Hubbell's fifty years as a trader, he owned twenty-four posts. Like other good traders, Hubbell "scrounged around" for markets for native crafts. He brought in Hispanic smiths to help local Navajos learn more about metalwork and encouraged weavers to shift from making blankets to rugs. Hubbell influenced the rug design that came to be known as Ganado, featuring a bold center diamond and distinctive deep red color. He produced a catalog of rugs for mail order sales and also sold rugs wholesale to the Fred Harvey Company and stores back East.

Above: The rug room at Hubbell Trading Post is a treasure trove of Navajo rugs and other crafts and artifacts, including the framed drawings for Hubbell's very first designs. *Right:* A Ganado-style rug. *Below:* A group of young Navajo men swear to serve their country as Code Talkers during WWII.

Movies in Monument Valley

To visitors seeing it for the first time, Monument Valley has a dreamlike déjà vu. And no wonder, the spires and buttes and mesas have been featured in numerous Western films and dozens of television commercials… and it all began with a rumor.

When local trader Harry Goulding heard a movie was to be filmed in the Flagstaff area, Harry persuaded photographer Joseph Muench to take several shots of Monument Valley scenery. He took the photos to Hollywood, where he convinced director John Ford that Monument Valley would not only make a perfect back-drop for his film, *Stagecoach*, but also help the Navajo people in a time of great need. The film, starring John Wayne, was the first of several Ford would make in the valley during the next three decades, inspiring many other directors to follow. Some familiar films:

Stagecoach (1939), John Ford
Fort Apache (1948), John Ford
She Wore a Yellow Ribbon (1949), John Ford
The Searchers (1956), John Ford
Sergeant Rutledge (1960), John Ford
Cheyenne Autumn (1964), John Ford
The Ten Commandments (1923), Cecil B. DeMille
2001: A Space Odyssey (1968), Stanley Kubrick
Easy Rider (1969), Dennis Hopper
The Eiger Sanction (1975), Clint Eastwood
National Lampoon's Vacation (1983), Harold Ramis
Back to the Future (1985), Robert Zemeckis
Forrest Gump (1994), Robert Zemeckis

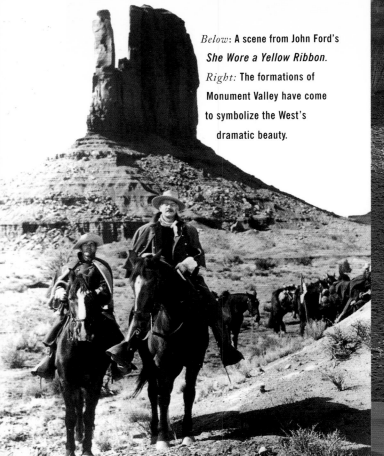

Below: A scene from John Ford's *She Wore a Yellow Ribbon.*
Right: The formations of Monument Valley have come to symbolize the West's dramatic beauty.

Diné Bikeyah: Navajo Country

Navajo landscape and culture are as tightly woven as a wool tapestry. Ni'hookáá' dine'é, the earth surface people, live between four sacred peaks: Sis Naajiní (Mt. Blanco) in the east, Tsoodził (Mt. Taylor) to the south, Dook'o'oosłííd (the San Francisco Peaks) to the west, and Dibé Nitsaa (Mt. Hesperus) in the north. The Diné emerged from four (some say three) previous worlds before entering this, the Fifth World. The holy people, Spider Woman, Talking God, and others, arranged four stones (black jet, white shell, turquoise, and abalone or coral) to mark tribal boundaries, and then placed sun, moon, and stars, and formed clouds, trees, rain, and other necessities.

But fierce monsters roamed the land, preying upon the Diné. Changing Woman's twin sons, Monster Slayer and Child-Born-of-Water, fought the monsters with lightning bolts, turning them to stone and shaping the landscape. Navajo chants describe earth's creation and instruct tribal members how to relate to each other and to the cosmos. Because illness is caused by being out of harmony with the world, traditional healers, hataałi, focus on chant and ceremony to bring the patient back into a state of balance. As one chant affirms, "It is finished in beauty."

After Hubbell died in 1930, debts, stock reductions, Depression, and war caused the family business to decline. In 1967, the National Park Service acquired the post and the Hubbell home, preserving the tradition of trade and hospitality that the Hubbell family began in 1883.

The greatest stronghold of Navajo tradition, both in the physical and spiritual sense, is in nearby Canyon de Chelly (pronounced "d'shay"), a network of deep canyons about fifty miles south of Four Corners. Though there's more than one explanation for how the canyon got its French-sounding name, the most common is that Spanish explorers transcribed the Navajo word "tségi," which roughly means "rock canyon," as Chegui or Chelly. But no matter

how it got its name, Canyon de Chelly holds much of the Southwest's history within its desert-varnished walls. Anasazi pueblos peer out from shadowy alcoves. The legendary Spider Woman, who taught the Navajo how to weave, lives at Spider Rock. Pictographs tell the story of Ute raids, and a trail leading up a cliff face reveals an escape route used to evade Kit Carson's soldiers.

The two main canyons, de Chelly (twenty-six miles long) and del Muerto (thirty-five miles long), are often referred to as South and North canyons respectively. The canyons are home to some fifty families, who cultivate small fields and graze sheep and goats. Though it is a national monument, the park service administers it in cooperation with canyon residents.

A paved road follows the north and south rims of the main canyons, with overlooks for Antelope House, Mummy Cave, and other ruins, as well as the slender eight-hundred-foot tall monolith Spider Rock. Visitors can hike the 2.5-mile (round trip) trail to White House ruin, an Anasazi village dating to A.D. 1060. To enter the canyon any other way, you must be accompanied by a guide. Local outfitters, including historic Thunderbird Lodge (built as a trading post in 1902), feature motorized and horseback tours of both canyons.

Above: Ship Rock is a place of legend, where Monster Slayer used an arrow of lightning to kill giant birds that preyed on the Navajo people. *Right:* A painting by Navajo artist Baje Whitethorne depicts the warrior twins. *Opposite:* Spider Rock, the home of Spider Woman, towers above the floor of Canyon de Chelly. *Pages 14-15:* Cottonwood trees turn gold along Chinle Wash, which flows through Canyon de Chelly after periods of rain.

The Art of Navajo Weaving

According to Navajo oral history, Spider Woman, who lives at the top of the spire named for her in Canyon de Chelly, taught women to weave. Because she is one of the Holy People, the art of weaving is imbued with reverence. Even today, a weaver may leave a break in her rug's design as a "spirit opening," much the way a spider's web has a hole in the center. Long ago, Navajo weavers did leave a small hole in the center of their blankets, as taught by Spider Woman. When traders refused to buy blankets with holes, weavers incorporated the opening into the design itself.

Traders also encouraged weavers to shift from blankets to rugs and to develop regional styles, such as the richly dyed Ganado Red, influenced by John Lorenzo Hubbell. Natural wool in shades of black, brown, and white was favored by trader J. B. Moore. He suggested bordered designs that led to the Two Grey Hills style, long known for its technical quality. At Wide Ruins Trading Post, Bill and Sallie Lippincott encouraged local weavers to use dyes made from native plants, resulting in the subtly toned Wide Ruins style, a banded design of horizontal patterns and stripes. On the western reservation, the popular Storm Pattern rug, depicting stylized mountains and lightning bolts, was probably influenced by a trader at Tuba City or Red Lake, and may even have been inspired by a flour sack design.

Around Shiprock, a hataałi (medicine man or singer) named Hosteen Klah began to weave the rare and controversial sandpainting-style rug, a pictorial design that duplicated sandpaintings used in healing ceremonies. Other pictorials include yeibichai (pronounced "yay-bachay") designs with dancers impersonating supernatural yeis, as well as scenes from nature or reservation life.

Today, with greater interaction and exchange between weavers, styles sometimes blend, and a weaver from Crystal might choose to create a Burntwater style rug. Innovations have been born, such as the raised outline technique used in New Lands designs. At the same time, traditional patterns, such as the chief blanket, are being revived. The variety and virtuosity of Navajo weaving guarantees that this three-hundred-year-old tradition will continue to engage collectors from around the world.

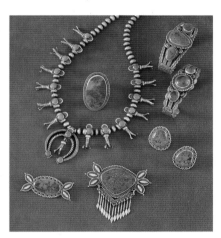

Opposite: A Monument Valley weaver instructs her daughter. *Above:* This collection of Navajo silver and turquoise includes a squash blossom necklace with naja pendant, a traditional design of Spanish influence. *Top right:* Window Rock, carved by wind from Cow Springs sandstone, is known as Tségháhoodzání, "perforated rock," in Navajo. *Right:* Navajo wedding baskets are traditionally coiled from sumac, with a break in the design called a "spirit line." This allows the weaver's creative energy to escape once she has completed the basket.

While Canyon de Chelly is the Navajos' spiritual center, the political center of the Navajo Nation lies to the southeast in Window Rock, Arizona. The population of the "Big Rez" is a quarter-million, making the Navajo the largest tribe in the country. Though herding continues to be important, tribal revenues stem from mineral resources, as well as from tourism. The Navajo Council House, shaped like a massive hogan, sits beneath the natural sandstone window.

A journey into Navajo land can encompass incredible scenery: the Little Colorado River gorge near Cameron; a historic trading post and gateway to Grand Canyon's East Rim; the colorful Hamblin Ridge and Echo Cliffs en route to the Gap; or the Painted Desert vistas near Tuba City. Quiet drives pass chapter houses, hogans, and herds of horses and sheep on the way to historic posts and "rug towns," such as Crystal, Two Grey Hills, or Teec Nos Pos.

Sheep were once the foundation of the Navajo economy, and weaving continues to be one of the most important arts. It is said that Spider Woman taught women how to weave on a loom made from sky and earth, with comb and spindles of white shell and lightning. Less romantically, anthropologists speculate that Navajo weavers learned from their Pueblo neighbors, beginning to use wool after the Spanish introduced sheep to the Southwest.

With continual innovation and increasing technical skill, Navajo weavers have elevated the rug to an art form. Contemporary weavings are so fine they are more accurately referred to as tapestries rather than rugs, with a yarn count greater than ninety per square inch.

Navajo silverwork has also continued to evolve. Some historians say the Navajos learned silversmithing at Bosque Redondo, although there are accounts of silver jewelry being worn on the Long Walk. At first, most silver was in the form of coinage; you might spot an old concha belt of heavy Mexican coins at a museum or in a trading post's special collection.

Turquoise is another cherished item that has long been treasured and traded among native peoples, evident by the beads and pendants found at ancient sites throughout the Southwest. But times are progressing even in terms of native art. Contemporary artisans of all Navajo crafts, including sandpainting, basketry, and pottery, are taking tradition into exciting new artistic territory.

Hopi
the Peaceful People

ACCORDING TO HOPI BELIEFS, their ancestors climbed up to this world on a reed. They were met by Masaaw, who told them to leave their footprints as they journeyed in search of the Center Place. They found it on the rocky fingers of First, Second, and Third mesas—long, high peninsulas extending outward from Black Mesa. People arrived from Homolovi, Chavez Pass, and elsewhere, settling on top of the mesas and below.

On arriving at the mesas, each group contributed a duty or ceremony to the community, creating cohesiveness among clans. Collectively, the Hopi are known as Hopituh Shinumo, the peaceful or well-mannered people. But life wasn't always peaceful.

Opposite: Walpi, a Hopi village occupied for more than three hundred years, is reached by a narrow peninsula of rock. *Above:* Susanna Denet wears a blanket shawl. *Below:* Crowds gather at a Hopi dance in 1911.

In 1540, members of Coronado's expedition ventured to the mesas, hoping the golden province described by the Zunis might offer riches. Hopi men drew a line of sacred cornmeal on the ground, but the Spanish crossed it. Later, New Spain sent colonists and priests, who established missions at all the pueblos. Priests entered kivas, destroying kachina masks, murals, and other ceremonial items and forced villagers to build churches. Finally, in 1680, nearly a hundred years before English colonists rebelled against British rule, the Pueblos rose up against the Spanish and defeated them.

Nearly two hundred years later, Anglo photographers, artists, and anthropologists "discovered" Hopi. Curious onlookers, some toting bulky box cameras on tripods, turned ceremonies into crowds. A few of the curious stayed. A joke among many southwestern tribes during the early 1900s went something like this: Describe a typical Indian family—a mother, father, three children, and an anthropologist.

In 1887, government interference in agriculture, education, and religion caused strife among the Hopi. Villages split between those who were "hostile" or "friendly" to the federal involvement, with Oraibi village at the center of the storm. Oraibi splintered, and factions moved to Hotevilla, Bacavi, Kykotsmovi, and Moenkopi. Many ceremonies closed to outsiders. Some ceremonies were lost as the number of clans dwindled. But still, Hopi remains the most traditional of all pueblos.

Today, there are a dozen villages on the mesas and below. Oraibi, established in 1150, is considered to be one of the oldest continuously inhabited settlements in the United States. It is located on Third Mesa, the farthest west. A good place to learn about Hopi ways is the cultural center on Second Mesa. Next door is a motel and a restaurant that features Hopi specialties.

You can also tour the traditional village of Walpi, perched on the very edge of First Mesa.

The Hopi calendar is divided between social and kachina ceremonials, the latter held from late December to July. If you are fortunate enough to visit during an open ceremony, remember that these are spiritual events, not displays. Photography and sketching are not permitted. Shrines near village plazas may hold feathers, plant shoots, pahos (prayer sticks), or other items and must not be disturbed. Think of the dances as prayers and as very special gifts: The Hopi pray for all the earth's peoples, not just for their own community.

The basket dances held by women's societies in September and October are often open to the public and feature one of the oldest art forms on the mesas. Baskets and plaques incorporate wicker weave, coil weave, and plaiting using local materials such as sumac, rabbitbrush, yucca, and galleta grass. Coiled and wicker plaques are especially colorful, with kachina figures or intricate geometric designs in natural and commercial dyes.

The kachina tradition dates back to ancestral sites, where the first stirrings of the kachina religion are seen in pottery designs and rock art imagery. The carving of wooden kachinas began as an educational tool to teach young children about these supernatural beings. Carving styles have changed through the years, particularly once collectors began to seek out various kachina styles and figures.

Opposite: Wicker plaques, woven on Third Mesa, come in a rainbow of colors and designs. *Above:* A pottery bowl has stylized feather and bird designs revived from sixteenth-century wares. *Right:* Hopi maidens sit on a housetop in 1921. *Below:* Shallow, wide-shouldered jars and a glossy sheen are characteristic of traditional Hopi pottery.

Pottery began to be used by Anasazi, Sinagua, and Mogollon ancestors when they settled in villages and raised food crops that required long simmering, such as beans. The first pottery was utilitarian and simple in design. As villages grew and skills became more specialized, pottery designs evolved and flourished. Today's Hopi pottery is still shaped by coiling and scraping, and then fired over open embers. It is exceptionally fine-walled, with intricate designs and a satiny finish.

Unlike their other art forms, the Hopi style of silverwork is a relatively recent innovation. Hopi men learned silversmithing in the late 1800s from Lanyade, a Zuni who was taught by a Navajo smith. The distinctive Hopi overlay style was suggested by Mary-Russell Colton, wife of Museum of Northern Arizona founder Harold Colton. She believed that by using symbols found on Hopi pottery, Hopi silversmiths could set their work apart from that of other tribes.

The idea took off after World War II, when returning GIs entered a training program to encourage employment on the Mesas. Artist Fred Kabotie was hired as a design teacher, and silversmith Paul Saufkie, Jr., taught technique. Hopi overlay uses two layers of silver, with a design cut into the top layer. The layers are soldered together and given either a polished or matte finish.

Kachinas: Benevolent Spirits

Kachinas are benevolent spirit beings that bring rain, food, health, and happiness to the Hopi people. Because the "ch" blend doesn't exist in the Hopi language, katsina is a more accurate spelling, though kachina is more widely used. The word can refer to the supernaturals, to the dancers who embody them in public ceremonies, and also to the wooden carvings.

Every year following the winter solstice, the kachinas return to the Hopi Mesas, making their first major public appearance in February during Powamu or Bean Dance, when Crow Mother presents corn kernels and bean sprouts to mark the beginning of another seasonal cycle. Ceremonies, dates, and openness to visitors vary from village to village, as do the kachinas.

More than three hundred different kachinas appear in ceremonies and are depicted in carvings. Kilts, shawls, headdresses, and body paint identify individuals, from the eagle-feather adorned hair of the Long-haired kachina to the black-and-white striped Koshari clowns of Hano village. Until the early 1900s, kachina dolls were flat, designed to hang on the walls of Hopi households and used to teach children about the supernaturals and the gifts they bring to the Hopi people. As collectors began purchasing kachinas, carvers began making dolls that could stand. After the 1940s, dolls were depicted in active poses and decorated with feathers. Due to government restrictions on using migratory bird feathers, some carvers after the 1970s began to carve feathers from wood. Sculpture-style dolls, often created from a single piece of cottonwood, have delicately carved feathers, fringe, and other details.

The wondrous panoply of kachinas, as well as the variety in carving styles, makes the dolls highly collectible. Each one is unique, and whether it is comic, scary, or graceful, it tells us something important about Hopi life and beliefs.

Opposite Top: The fearsome-looking Hú or
Whipper Kachina appears in February at the
Bean Dance (Powamu) and is responsible for
initiating children into the kachina society.
Opposite Bottom: Traditional Kachinas from
Left to Right: Ma'lo, Paiyata-um, Sa-Qua Hote,
Navuk'china, Sio Hemis, Muyingua, and Toson
Koyemsi. *Above:* Symbolism used in overlay
jewelry includes corn, kachinas, clouds, rain,
feathers, and water. To the Hopi, these symbols have layers of significance that go beyond
their simple graphic beauty. *Below:* The
delicate feathers and fringe of this dancing
Eagle kachina (Kwahu) are skillfully carved
from cottonwood root.

Not far from the modern-day Hopi Mesas
are several places where the "footsteps"—ruined
villages, rock writing, and pottery sherds—of
the Hisatsinom, or ancestors, can be seen.
Sandal Trail offers hawk's-eye views of
Betatakin, which can also be visited on a steep,
five-mile roundtrip, ranger-led hike. A circular
white pictograph marks the canyon wall near
the cliff dwelling. Some say it is a Hopi clan
symbol, signifying the Fire Clan or indicating
Masaaw, who gave fire to the Hisatsinom when
they entered the Fourth World.

Keet Seel, perhaps the most exquisitely preserved ancestral dwelling in Arizona, lies eight
miles down canyon. It can be reached on foot
or via horseback in the company of a guide.
The journey, though long, is a good way to
leave the modern world behind. Only twenty
people each day may enter Keet Seel in small
ranger-led groups.

South of the Hopi Mesas, along the margins
of the Little Colorado River, crops grew even
during drought times. Because of this, people
settled and resettled the hilltop pueblos known
as Homolovi. For some ancestral Puebloan
clans, this was the last stopping place on the
journey to the center of the world. A lonely

place, Homolovi was targeted by pothunters
until former governor Bruce Babbitt designated
it as a state park in 1986.

Further west along the Little Colorado,
Wupatki National Monument preserves several
villages with multicultural traits. Some archaeologists believe that the volcanic eruption of
nearby Sunset Crater sparked immigration,
drawing Kayenta Anasazi, Cohonina, and Sinagua
farmers, who raised crops in soil covered with
volcanic cinders.

Excavations indicate a vast trade network, with macaws, copper bells, eighty pottery styles, and shell jewelry from as far away as the Pacific.

East of Flagstaff, Walnut Canyon National Monument is one of the loveliest ancestral sites in the Four Corners region. As at Wupatki, population increased here after Sunset Crater's eruption, only to drop sharply during the mid-1200s. This deep, narrow canyon once sheltered the Sinagua, who built homes into the limestone ledges high above Walnut Creek.

On the northern edge of Flagstaff below the lava dome of Mt. Elden lies Elden Pueblo, a village the Hopi call Pasiovi, meaning "the place of coming together." The Sinagua, Hopi ancestors, lived here until about A.D. 1275. Hopi

oral traditions claim that this pueblo was a place where people from other villages would gather to take part in ceremonial activities.

Intrigued by potsherds they found while picnicking near Elden Pueblo and horrified by the numbers of artifacts that were being excavated and sent off to Eastern museums, Harold and Mary Colton launched the Museum of Northern Arizona (MNA). Harold became the first to identify the Sinagua culture, and Mary launched an MNA tradition, the annual Hopi Market, bringing Hopi artists and dancers to the museum's grounds every summer. The tradition has expanded to include markets featuring Hispanic, Navajo, Zuni, and Pai art.

Left: The Sinaguan ruins of steep-sided Walnut Canyon are tucked into layers of limestone. *Above:* The empty rooms and walkways of Keet Seel, an Anasazi village, seem almost haunted. *Opposite:* The alcove at Betatakin shelters over a hundred rooms above a pocket forest of aspen and fir.

the Lands

Many who visit the Four Corners find themselves transformed by its stark beauty. This is a landscape stripped bare by the forces of nature, crossed by powerful rivers that cut deep canyons from layer upon layer of colorful stone. Snowy peaks and expansive mesas stack up on the horizon in hues of blue, lavender, green, and gray. Sandstone, limestone, and shale form cliff walls and standing rocks. Everywhere, wind and water have sculpted wildly shaped pinnacles, hoodoos, and arches.

Here you'll find sparse high desert, thick stands of ponderosa, and everything in between. Cactus and lizards live side-by-side with elk and mountain lion. The coyote roams it all, inspiring legends about his boldness and ego. Coyote, it is said, scattered the chips of mica that First Man and First Woman had set aside to create the heavens, and indeed, night skies are crowded with stars so brilliant they seem close enough to touch.

Day or night, the air is clear and dry, scented with sage, pine, and saltbush. Sunshine predominates, though seasonal thunderstorms briefly buffet the land with lightning and rain. Seeds have learned to bide their time. Wildflowers burst into red, yellow, and purple after summer storms and winter showers. Slow-growing junipers, centuries old, cling to bare rock, their roots seeking soil and moisture.

The Four Corners region, one of the last in the U.S. to be mapped, still imparts a sense of discovery, inviting exploration of its national preserves, forests, and tribal parks. It is a place of wonder, where the ancient past seems near, where life clings with tenacity, where the land itself is inextricably woven into story and legend.

Left: Grand Canyon explorer John Wesley Powell named this area the Vermilion Cliffs for its brilliantly colored sandstones.
Above: Lake Powell's Padre Bay, as seen from Cookie Jar Butte.

Arizona
Ancient Volcanoes *and* Stone Forests

Throughout the Moenkopi, worm tubes, raindrop patterns, ammonite fossils, and reptile tracks hint at ancient life.

After the seaway receded, lakes and rivers deposited softly colored mudstones and siltstones in glorious shades of gray, lavender, white, pink, salmon, and green. These deposits eroded into the colorful slopes of the Painted Desert, a crescent-shaped swath across northern Arizona from Tuba City to Holbrook.

Wood drifted along the ancient rivers, its cellular structure slowly filled in by fine silica, turning it to stone. Prehistoric people used petrified wood to make arrow points and pueblos. At Petrified Forest National Park, a small Anasazi ruin with walls of petrified wood, called Agate House, dates to A.D. 1150.

Opposite: According to Navajo legend, the fallen stone trees of Petrified Forest National Park are the bones of a monster who was destroyed by the sun. *Top right:* Stone logs lie scattered in a wash near Petrified Forest's Blue Mesa. *Above and bottom right:* Through the ages, wind has sculpted the colorful sandstone of the Paria Canyon–Vermilion Cliffs Wilderness Area.

THE DOMINANT LANDFORM OF THE Four Corners is the Colorado Plateau, a 130,000-square mile upland that covers the northeastern half of Arizona and stretches into Utah, Colorado, and New Mexico. This high tableland was once the basin of a tropical inland sea. Along the southern edge of the Colorado Plateau, ancient swamps, a meteor crater, and the lava flows of a volcanic field are testaments to the forces that slowly shaped the Four Corners area. During Triassic times, 250 million years ago, tidal flats and mud banks formed the reddish brown mudstones and siltstones known as the Moenkopi Formation, named for the Hopi village of Moenkopi.

As trees turned to stone over millions of years, sand dunes, sea floor, and mud became sandstone, limestone, and shale. Then, about ten million years ago, a great upheaval lifted these sedimentary deposits, forcing the earth's crust to buckle and swell. Rivers cut into the uplifted plateau, forming deep, steep-walled canyons—including Arizona's Grand Canyon, Glen Canyon, and Canyon de Chelly.

Beginning about six million years ago and lasting up until the last millennium, northern Arizona rumbled with volcanoes. The San Francisco Peaks volcanic field covered two thousand square miles. The Peaks themselves were once a single huge volcano, formed by successive layers of lava. Geologists theorize that a half-million years ago, the volcano erupted and collapsed, forming a series of peaks, including distinctive Agassiz and Humphreys, sacred to both Navajo and Hopi tribes. At 12,663 feet, Humphreys Peak is the highest point in Arizona, visible more than a hundred miles away.

Above and Right: Grand Canyon National Park's less-visited North Rim offers stunning views of Mt. Hayden and Marble Canyon *(above)* and Cape Royal *(right).*

The volcanic field that covers northern Arizona includes some six hundred cinder cones, which are rounded or pyramid-shaped peaks formed from droplets of erupting lava. One cinder cone, Sunset Crater, is believed to have first erupted in A.D. 1065. The glow in the sky must have been visible for hundreds of miles, a possible factor in the population explosion that occurred at nearby Wupatki. In the 1920s, a movie company had its eye on the crater, hoping to dynamite it and film the resulting explosion for a dramatic scene. But Museum of Northern Arizona founder Harold Colton came to the rescue, and Sunset Crater gained national monument status.

Today, visitors can get a closer look at fumaroles (gas vents), lava tubes, and an ice cave (similar to ones Flagstaff saloons harvested ice from in the 1880s). Along the thirty-six mile scenic loop road from Sunset Crater to Wupatki, Bonito Park offers lovely vistas of the crater, with meadows of sunflowers and Indian paintbrush.

Lava flows sometimes formed dams and lakes. Thousands of years ago, a lava flow dammed the Little Colorado River at Grand Falls. Lava from nearby Merriam Crater filled the two-hundred-foot deep canyon. The Little Colorado piled up sediment behind the lava dam, forcing the river to meander east around the flow, where horizontal layers of softer Kaibab limestone subsequently eroded into steep steps. During spring runoff in March and April, the river plunges down the steps in a muddy torrent into the canyon below.

Forces even greater than Earth's mark the landscape between Flagstaff and Winslow. Forty-nine thousand years ago, an eighty-ton meteor of nickel and iron hurtled from space and crashed into the plateau thirty-five miles east of Flagstaff. The violent impact left a crater a mile wide and six hundred feet deep—room enough for twenty football fields or a stadium for two million fans. Visitors can hike the three-mile trail around the rim of Meteor Crater to get a sense of the magnitude of this collision between Earth and space.

Nearby, the relatively flat Little Colorado River valley made a natural route for those who were first to explore territory ceded to the United States by Mexico. Surveyors, geologists, and soldiers crossed here seeking minerals, grazing lands, and a route to California.

Above: Wildflowers change with the seasons in the meadows of Bonita Park below Sunset Crater. *Below:* A summer thunderstorm builds over Agassiz, Fremont, and Humphreys peaks, an extinct volcanic range collectively known as the San Francisco Peaks.

Opposite Top: The sediment-laden springtime flow of the Little Colorado River tumbles nearly two hundred feet at Grand Falls.

Opposite Bottom: Astronauts once trained at the lunar landscape of Meteor Crater.

Pages 34-35: The San Francisco Peaks, winter home of the kachinas, rise behind Lomaki ruin at Wupatki National Monument.

Lt. Edward F. Beale led one notable expedition in 1853, plotting a wagon road along the thirty-fifth parallel. Beale also led twenty-five camels imported from Asia, an army experiment to see if they would fare better than horses in the high desert. The camel experiment failed miserably, but his wagon road was a success.

The Prescott–Santa Fe Stage Line followed part of Beale's route, and later so did the Atlanta & Pacific Railroad. The major obstacle to travel was Diablo Canyon, named by Spanish explorers who found it devilish to cross. In 1882, the A&P crossed the canyon with an iron bridge more than five hundred feet long.

She also decorated the nearby Painted Desert Inn at Petrified Forest National Park and created several buildings at Grand Canyon. La Posada was her favorite. Train travelers could step from its graceful archways onto one of Fred Harvey Company's Indian Detours, journeying to the Hopi Mesas and other destinations in Packard touring cars or Cadillacs, guided by "couriers," attractive young women wearing vented skirts, velveteen blouses, cloche hats, and Indian jewelry.

But Depression, war, and the family motor-car put an end to train travel. La Posada went on the auction block in 1957. Colter lamented, "There's such a thing as living too long." If only she could see her masterpiece now. The residents of Winslow have lovingly restored La Posada, and today the hotel's gracious atmosphere recalls the days of elegant travel.

In 1926, the National Trails Highway, once Beale's wagon road, became Route 66. The Great Mother Road led dust bowl refugees west to California. Later, families traveled it as America's Main Street, the downtown thoroughfare of small communities throughout the West. Bright neon signs beckoned across the dark desert, advertising cafés, curio shops, and motels. Many of the signs still stand, and so do a few sections of Route 66 pavement in towns like Flagstaff and Seligman, Arizona. Though change is certain, some things endure forever, such as the sense of adventure and promise of the exotic found along this long-traveled corridor.

Holbrook and Winslow sprang up along the rails as cattle shipping points, though Winslow was said to be the more respectable of the two, with a hospital and library. Holbrook was a "rowdy cow town," for awhile the only church-less county seat in the U.S.

As the Santa Fe Railway pushed west, a new era of elegant travel began. The Fred Harvey Company opened dining establishments along the rail lines, followed by hotels with Spanish, Western, and Indian themes. No one could create atmosphere quite like company architect and designer Mary Colter, who frequently sought input from Fred Kabotie and other Native American artists.

In Winslow, Colter designed an elegant Spanish Colonial resort named La Posada.

Top Left: Route 66 neon continues to welcome travelers to Flagstaff and other Western towns. *Top Right:* Dilophosaurus track. *Below:* Harvey Car tours were once an elegant and adventurous way to explore the region. *Opposite:* The Painted Desert's softly eroded, multicolored slopes were deposited by ancient lakes and rivers.

Ancient Life

During the Jurassic Age, about 200 million years ago, dinosaurs roamed the swampy lowlands of northern Arizona. About five miles west of Tuba City on the Navajo Reservation, tracks of large carnivorous reptiles are preserved in stone.

Evidence of even older lifeforms can be seen east of Holbrook at Petrified Forest National Park, where fish, amphibians, and reptiles formed a primordial ecosystem. The remains of a primitive dinosaur nicknamed Gertie, discovered in 1984, still puzzle paleontologists. The park is a repository of ancient life, most notably the large trees that slowly turned to stone over the ages.

This treasure trove of geologic and cultural history tempted early settlers, who hauled off petrified wood by wagonloads. Horrified locals sought protection from Congress, and in 1906, Theodore Roosevelt signed legislation that set aside more than sixty thousand acres as a national monument, protecting ruins, rock art, and fossils along with the fallen stone forests. Today, the park's scenic drives, trails, and overlooks encompass breathtaking views of the Painted Desert and offer up-close looks at petrified logs, Anasazi pueblos, and the Painted Desert Inn, once a travelers' oasis along old Route 66.

In 1540, the viceroy dispatched an expedition led by Francisco Vásquez de Coronado. When

Pueblo Pottery

Some nineteen hundred years ago, Ancestral Puebloans combined the elements of earth, water, and fire to make pottery. These ancient wares have helped archaeologists develop a continuous timeline that identifies trade and settlement patterns in the Southwest. Remarkably, the Puebloans' labor-intensive art survived Spanish and American influence. When collectors began to buy pottery in the early 1900s, the craft underwent a renaissance led by Nampeyo, a Tewa woman from Hopi, Maria of San Ildefonso, and others. Today, Pueblo and Navajo potters sell their wares throughout the Four Corners area.

From Taos to the southern Rio Grande Pueblos and west to Acoma, Laguna, Zuni, and Hopi, potters have developed distinct styles, from the deeply carved black-on-black of Santa Clara to the astonishingly detailed geometric designs of Acoma. The subtle sparkle of micaceous pottery from Taos is all natural, pure and simple, while the polychromes of Zuni and Zia are elaborately decorated with birds, deer, frogs, and other creatures. Perhaps the most traditional ware comes from Hopi, with stylized feathers, birds, and geometric designs inspired by sixteenth-century sherds.

The most traditional wares are handmade in multitude of steps that include gathering local clay, shaping by coiling and scraping or pinching, decorating with mineral or vegetable paints, and then firing outdoors in a wood or dung fire. Common shapes include wide-shouldered jars, seed pots, twin-necked wedding vases, canteens, and bowls, as well as such unusual forms as Cochiti's storytellers and Zuni's fetish pots. The elements that go into these designs are difficult to control, resulting in uniqueness but also increasing the risk of loss, making pottery highly collectible, as well as expensive. But pottery enthusiasts will tell you that a pot is not only a physical representation of its maker's time and great skill, but also a link that extends back centuries to the very first potters, whose work continues to teach us about this land's first permanent residents.

Left: The legacy of Pueblo pottery began centuries ago with Anasazi potters, who crafted the three large black-on-white jars below.

Maize

The Zuni word for corn, dowa, also means "ancient." Thousands of years ago, a New World grass called teosinte began to evolve with human help into Zea mays. By selecting seeds, humans influenced genetic change, and resulting strains of maize varied according to soil type and climate. With corn agriculture, the ancients' way of life changed from nomadic hunting and gathering to settled villages. Life-sustaining corn developed a spiritual element. At Hopi, corn's growing cycle is inextricably connected to the human cycle of life.

Corn is sacred also to the Navajo, who use corn pollen or cornmeal in many ceremonies. In a traditional wedding, bride and groom each take pinches of cornmeal from a basket, which is then passed to guests.

Feast days feature corn food, such as Hopi piki bread made from blue corn, and posole, a rich stew made with hominy, which is corn with the hull and germ removed. Corn symbols adorn silver jewelry and are woven into rugs. Even the landscape honors the Southwest's most important plant at Dowa Yallane, Corn Mountain, which rises east of Zuni Pueblo, and at Hopi, where the Corn Twins stand like sentinels on Second Mesa.

More than eight decades later, tribes from as far away as Mexico City and Oklahoma participate in the Ceremonial's art show, dances, rodeo, and parades with dazzling displays of traditional regalia. The warm, friendly gathering and its blend of cultures is quintessentially Western, and is held every August beneath the sweeping sandstone mesas surrounding Red Rock State Park.

The same year the Ceremonial began, the Fred Harvey Company announced it had budgeted three-quarters of a million dollars to build a hotel on the Santa Fe Railroad line. El Navajo's grand opening in 1923 was attended by two thousand Indians from various tribes. Today, on the former site of the hotel, Gallup's cultural center hosts beautiful native dance performances.

Hollywood also came to Gallup to film *Texas Rangers*, *The Streets of Laredo*, and other Westerns. Stars slept at the elegant El Rancho,

built by the brother of movie director D. W. Griffith. Photos of guests Ronald Reagan, Jimmy Stewart, and others hang in the second floor mezzanine. The grand old hotel, restored by local trader Armand Ortega, showcases Indian art and Western furnishings.

North of town, Hwy. 666 passes sheep farms and chapter houses on its way to Shiprock, following the edge of the Chuska Mountains. A break in the range near Sheep Springs commemorates a skirmish between the Navajo and Lt. Col. John Washington's troops, during which the Navajo leader Narbona was shot to death. One of a handful of respected leaders, the elderly Narbona was admired for the brave exploits of his youth, as well as for his efforts to seek peace for his people before he died. This area was known as Washington Pass until students from Navajo Community College in Tsaile successfully argued to have the name changed to Narbona Pass.

For miles, the seventeen-hundred-foot volcanic vent called Ship Rock appears to float on the horizon like a double-masted ghost ship. The Navajo call it Tsé bit'a'í, Winged Rock, and consider it sacred ground. Fifteen miles to the northeast is the town of Shiprock. The largest city on the reservation, it is home to several fine trading posts, including the Shiprock Trading Post and Foutz Trading Company.

Top left: Inlay jewelry is a Zuni specialty. *Left:* Route 66 in historic Gallup. *Above:* Hopi farmers raise corn in a rainbow of colors. *Opposite:* The salmon-colored cliffs of Red Rock State Park make a dramatic backdrop for

Opposite: Ship Rock's jagged basalt cliffs are the neck of an extinct volcano. *Top:* A hawk's eye view of Pueblo Bonito, a Chaco Canyon great house, reveals the circular walls of more than thirty kivas or ceremonial spaces. *Above:* Visitors can walk through a maze of connecting rooms at Aztec Ruins National Monument. *Right:* The restored great kiva at Aztec ruins once reverberated with the sights and sounds of dancers and spectators.

This area is known for sandpaintings and the rugs they inspired. Weavers at nearby Teec Nos Pos create spectacular bordered rugs said to be influenced by the Oriental rugs popular in Victorian parlors.

East of Shiprock, the San Juan, Animas, and La Plata rivers join in a fertile valley that attracted farmers and ranchers in the 1870s. Town names like Farmington, Fruitland, and Bloomfield hint at the area's agricultural history. Peel back the layers of history and you will find a rich prehistory. Local farmers did just that, uncovering artifacts, walls, and sometimes entire villages as they plowed.

Aztec Ruins National Monument preserves a 450-room pueblo along the banks of the Animas, the river of souls. Standing beneath the canopy of cottonwoods on a quiet fall afternoon, it is easy to imagine the potters, jewelers, weavers, and children who lived in this three-story village.

At the last millennium's dawning, Anasazi life centered in Chaco Canyon, about sixty-five miles south of Aztec. Because Anasazi is a Navajo word that means "enemy ancestors," many archaeologists prefer the term Ancestral Puebloan to describe these prehistoric farmers, who occupied the Four Corners area until about 1300. During their time at Chaco, the Anasazi built massive kivas and multistoried pueblos and also crafted finely decorated black-on-white pottery and turquoise jewelry. A network of

straight roads led in all directions to "outliers," other large pueblos built in the Chacoan style, including Aztec and nearby Salmon Ruins.

When Earl Morris excavated Aztec beginning in 1916, he discovered the village had been abandoned and then reoccupied by people fleeing Mesa Verde. In the 1930s, Morris began to reconstruct Aztec's great kiva, the largest restored kiva in existence. The roof, at eighteen hundred square feet, is made of log beams and a foot-thick layer of earth, and is estimated to weigh ninety tons. In keeping with prehistoric building methods, no nails or pegs were used.

In nearby Bloomfield, the three hundred room pueblo known today as Salmon Ruins was once the homestead of a Mormon family named Salmon. Pueblo walls feature the thin stone slabs and precise masonry of the Chacoans. Like neighboring Aztec, this village was constructed as a Chacoan-style great house around A.D. 1100 and abandoned by 1150. The village stood deserted for a century before being briefly reoccupied by the Mesa Verdeans. They subdivided the large Chaco-style rooms and added several kivas.

The great mystery of the "vanishing" Anasazi civilizations is not where they went, but why they left. Abandoned cliff dwellings and pueblos once gave rise to a popular belief that an entire race had vanished, but today we understand that the ancient ones moved to Hopi, Zuni, and the Rio Grande Valley, where their descendants live today. Perhaps crowded villages depleted the resources around them, forcing migration. The residents of Salmon and Aztec likely moved eastward to the Rio Grande pueblos, continuing traditions begun centuries ago.

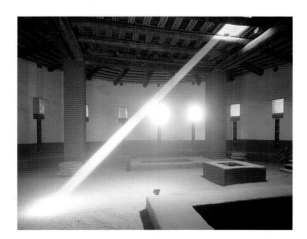

Colorado
Mountains, Mesas, *and* Canyons

One struck gold in the San Juan Mountains and managed to keep the secret for two years. But word leaked out, and by 1873, prospectors had staked four thousand claims in southwestern Colorado. For 12 cents an acre and the promise of peace, Chief Ouray was persuaded to give up tribal lands. The gold boom was on.

Miners required food, so cattlemen moved in to provide it. The Wetherills, a ranching family who arrived in Mancos Valley in 1880, became more interested in searching around their Alamo Ranch for Indian ruins than in chasing cows. Al Wetherill was first to see "what seemed like a small ruined city." His brother Richard and brother-in-law Charlie Mason spotted the city again in December 1888 while searching for cattle on a mesa above Cliff Canyon. As snow gently fell, they stopped to rest their horses at the mesa's edge and looked across the canyon to see a deep alcove. Within, like a deserted castle, was an extensive village.

They scrambled down the mesa using tree limbs and ropes, and then climbed the other side of the canyon to reach Cliff Palace, Wetherill's name for the village. Over the next day and a half they found two more large villages, Spruce Tree House and Square Tower House. Two years later, the Wetherills had searched through nearly two hundred ruins in the Mesa Verde area and turned their ranch into a small museum.

In 1891, a young Swede named Gustaf Nordenskiöld saw the Wetherills' collections and decided to make a detailed description of Mesa Verde's sites. He hired John Wetherill as his foreman. The other four Wetherill brothers helped dig when they could free themselves from ranch chores. Unfortunately, Nordenskiöld took the artifacts he collected back to Europe, outraging locals, who pressured the government to protect Mesa Verde. In 1906 Theodore Roosevelt signed the Antiquities Act, making it illegal to remove artifacts from public land.

Opposite: **An overlook offers a stunning view of Square Tower House at Mesa Verde National Park.** *Above:* **A group of Hopi Eagle Dancers perform at Mesa Verde.** *Right:* **The remarkable fine-line decoration of this centuries-old Anasazi jar was probably done with a yucca leaf brush and vegetal paint.**

For NEARLY THREE CENTURIES, Spain explored and colonized the Four Corners Region, leaving names like Sierra de la Plata, Rio Mancos, and Mesa Verde. The Old Spanish Trail, which weaves its way through the Four Corners, was mapped by Dominguez and Escalante, a pair of Spanish priests seeking a route to California. They passed through the area in 1776, the year the American Revolution began. Later, the Utes became the Native American version of highwaymen, stopping traders and demanding a toll from those who traveled the Old Spanish Trail through their territory, which included half of present-day Colorado and much of Utah.

Ute bands once ranged over a large area seeking plants and game. After acquiring horses, they hunted bison, lived in tepees, and became fierce raiders. But after gold was discovered on the other side of the Rockies, prospectors spilled over the Continental Divide into Ute territory.

Three weeks later, Mesa Verde became a national park.

Today, Mesa Verde National Park is the largest park dedicated to preserving the nation's prehistoric treasures. Its two mesas, Chapin and Wetherill, encompass some four thousand sites, with evidence of human use going back at least fourteen hundred years. About six hundred sites are cliff dwellings, the most ever found in one locale. The park is open year-round, though access to particular sites changes with the season. Make your first stop Far View Visitor Center, where rangers will arrange tours of Cliff Palace and Balcony House, available by reservation only.

These and other Chapin Mesa sites are the most popular and accessible. The mesa's museum has displays and artifacts that help recreate Anasazi life at Mesa Verde. Spruce Tree House, the park's third largest village, features a reconstructed kiva. At Balcony House, ladders and a narrow passageway add to the sense of discovery. Cliff Palace, the largest ruin, and the one most people picture when they think of southwestern prehistory, has 217 rooms and 23 kivas. Like most of Mesa Verde's cliff dwellings, this village was occupied for less than a hundred years before being abandoned.

For those who yearn to explore the Anasazi world without modern-world crowds, Ute Mountain Tribal Park, "the other Mesa Verde," is literally next door. The tribal park's 125,000 acres border Mesa Verde National Park on three sides, and its settlements are actually a continuation of the Mesa Verdean communities. Together, the two parks include a series of mesas cut from north to south by more than twenty deep canyons. All of the canyons drain into the Mancos River, which begins on the La Plata Mountain's west slopes and flows toward the San Juan River.

Ruins perched within the tribal park's Lion Canyon can be visited with a Ute guide. Lion House is the canyon's largest ruin at forty rooms. Archaeologist Earl Morris uncovered a hundred sandals here—all unworn. He also excavated the village called Morris No. 5. It had a pen for turkeys, valued for their feathers, which the Anasazi knotted into warm blankets. A ladder leads to Eagle Nest House, where one kiva has a fairly intact mural.

Rock art in Mancos Canyon includes Anasazi petroglyphs of geometric designs and humanlike forms, as well as Ute pictographs of horses. A particularly large panel is near the former home of Jack House, the last traditional chief of the Ute Mountain Utes and the originator of public tours. Half- and full-day driving tours, and guided backpacking trips are available.

Cowboy Archaeologists

For archaeology buffs, no fantasy is as powerful as that of finding an ancient city lost to the world. When the Wetherill brothers found Mesa Verde, the experience changed their lives. For the next several decades, these cowboys turned archaeologists explored and recorded prehistoric sites from Mesa Verde to Keet Seel to Chaco Canyon.

Hoping others would share their enthusiasm, the Wetherills displayed artifacts in Colorado towns. But for many, conflicts with the Utes were recent memories, and in this age of new discoveries, more people looked to the future than the past. "We were too young and inexperienced to know when we were licked," Al Wetherill wrote.

Working with a young Swede named Gustaf Nordenskiöld at Mesa Verde, the Wetherills learned careful excavation techniques and rudimentary stratigraphy, the idea that cultural material is deposited oldest on the bottom and newest on the top. The Wetherills kept notes on each site they explored and were among the first to use a camera to record excavations. Richard often spoke with local Indians, gathering ethnographic information to help answer his questions about artifacts, a practice later used by other archaeologists.

Richard and John Wetherill stayed involved in archaeology the rest of their lives. In 1910, Richard was murdered at Chaco Canyon, where he is buried. John established trading posts in Monument Valley and led expeditions into the Southwest's remote corners until he was an old man. Fred Blackburn, former BLM ranger and Wetherill historian, credits the brothers for introducing the world to "the archaeological riches of the Four Corners."

Opposite: **Square Tower House is a cliff dwelling of seventy rooms and seven kivas.**
Above: **Eagle Nest House perches high on a canyon wall in Ute Mountain Tribal Park.**
Below: **Lowry Pueblo, constructed about A.D. 1060, encompasses forty rooms and eight kivas, including a large kiva with a painted mural.**

The tribe operates two campgrounds and a casino south of Cortez. The Ute Mountain Utes make decorative slipcast ware at a nearby pottery factory. The tribal museum in Montrose features a traditional Ute dwelling and an interpretation of the Ute's annual Bear Dance. The Southern Ute branch operates a casino and cultural center in Ignacio. Ute leather goods and beadwork can be found in trading posts in Ignacio, Mancos, and Cortez.

The farming and ranching community of Cortez, founded in 1887, is the pinto bean capitol of the world. It's also the gateway to Mesa Verde, with dozens of motels and trading posts.

On summer evenings, Native American dances are held at the cultural center downtown. For those who want to do more than just explore, the Crow Canyon Archaeological Center offers programs and workshops on excavation and laboratory research, teaching hands-on techniques for a day, a week, or longer.

North of Cortez, the lovely town of Dolores lies along one of the Southwest's best trout streams. Locals and visitors also head for McPhee reservoir, the second largest lake in Colorado, to fish, boat, and camp. On its shores, the Bureau of Land Management (BLM) operates the Anasazi Heritage Center. The museum houses over three million artifacts, focusing on the area's prehistory as well as Ute, Navajo, and pioneer life. Hands-on activities include weaving on a Navajo loom and grinding corn with a metate and mano. Ruins named for the Spanish explorers Dominguez and Escalante are just a short hike away.

The BLM also manages the Canyons of the Ancients National Monument, established in 2000 by President Clinton. The monument's 163,000 acres incorporate the ruins of Hovenweep and Lowry Pueblo, where eight kivas hint at a busy community life. It's a reminder that cultures flourish and fade, leaving behind ruined villages and ghost towns, with names on a map, flakes of stone, or fragments of pottery to tell their stories.

Utah
The End *of the* Rainbow

Opposite: **The ancient ones left signs of their passing throughout southern Utah.**
Above: **The Anasazi built their homes among Monument Valley's dramatic spires and buttes.** *Right:* **A full moon rises over Monument Valley, silhouetting the slender monolith known as Totem Pole.**

T HOUGH ONE OF THE LAST PLACES in the U.S. to be mapped, humans have occupied Utah's diverse lands for centuries. Fremont and Anasazi sheltered in sandstone canyons, which were later roamed by Ute and Navajo horsemen. Still later, it was the promised land of Mormon pioneers, a place to settle in peace and prosperity.

But the story that dominates all others here is geology. Sedimentary sandstone and limestone, stripped by erosion and shaped by uplift, form stark hogbacks and hoodoos, as well as the fabulous standing rocks of Monument Valley. Rivers carved deep canyons and corkscrew slots. Long-ago volcanoes created the skyline's La Sal and Abajo mountains.

Utah's magnificent scenery is preserved in a dozen national parks and monuments, with Arches, Canyonlands, Capitol Reef, and Grand Staircase–Escalante easily reached from Blanding, Monticello,

or Moab. The oldest of Utah's public preserves is Natural Bridges National Monument, set aside by Theodore Roosevelt in 1908 to protect three natural spans of Cedar Mesa sandstone cut by intermittently flowing streams in White Canyon. Because they are formed by water erosion, these stone spans are called "bridges," differentiating them from the "arches" at Arches National Park, which were created by wind erosion.

After gaining monument status, the bridges were bestowed with Hopi names: Sipapu, Kachina, and Owachomo. Though the Hopi didn't live here, some of their ancestors did, leaving rock writing near Kachina bridge and building stone pueblos throughout this corner of the state. During the 1200s, Hovenweep's villagers built remarkable square, oval, circular, and D-shaped towers. Archaeologists have speculated about the towers' defensive nature or use as celestial observatories. Because they are contemporaneous with European castles, village names have a heraldic ring: Hovenweep Castle, Square Tower, Stronghold House.

Hovenweep, Ute for deserted valley, was named by two members of the 1874 Hayden expedition, photographer William Henry Jackson and zoologist Ernest Ingersoll. It is a lonely place, abandoned at the end of the thirteenth century and free from crowds today. It straddles the Utah-Colorado border, with visitor center and campground on the Utah side. Many of the local roads are gravel, accessible to passenger cars unless the weather is wet. The route entering from the west passes Hatch Trading Post, a graceful adobe built in 1903 among cliffs and cottonwoods. The southern route goes through Aneth, a Navajo town named for a trader whose business practices were aneth, or "like the devil's."

A Rainbow of Stone

John Wetherill, Mesa Verde's cowboy archaeologist, established Oljeto Trading Post in Monument Valley but never lost his thirst for exploring. "Hosteen John" heard about a vast stone bridge from his Navajo neighbors and from Paiute Nasja Begay. The Paiute people call the bridge Barohoini, "the rainbow upon which one could travel to the sun." The Navajo consider Tsé'naanání'áhí a symbol of the yei, supernaturals that create clouds, rain, and rainbows.

Nasja Begay and Wetherill led the famed 1909 expedition to Rainbow Bridge, and Wetherill outfitted and guided subsequent expeditions. Eroded from Navajo sandstone, Rainbow Bridge is the largest natural bridge in the world, rising over three hundred feet above the canyon floor and stretching nearly three hundred feet wide. In 1910, President Taft proclaimed it a national monument.

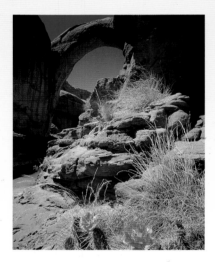

Above and Right: Rainbow Bridge, fifty water miles from Lake Powell's popular marinas, once sheltered an ancestral puebloan shrine and a Navajo altar. It was also the setting for Zane Grey's novel *The Rainbow Trail.*

Blanding, the largest town in San Juan County, was settled as Sidon in 1905, mostly by Mormon farmers washed out by floods at Bluff. A small-town sensibility is preserved here along with many historic buildings. Blanding's friendly hospitality includes inns, B&Bs, and a long tradition of hosting those who come to explore the area's many ruins. The one hundred mile, mostly paved scenic drive called Trail of the Ancients connects prehistoric sites. Archaeology buffs can also float down the San Juan, back-pack into Grand Gulch, or arrange for a tour by horseback or llama.

The first historic settlement in this corner of Utah was Bluff, founded in 1880. The city's historic loop passes a dozen Victorian-era homes as well as Indian ruins and rock art. Beneath a pair of rock hoodoos on the north end of town is Twin Rocks Trading Post, where Navajo baskets, folk art, pottery, and rugs can be found. Also north of town, Cow Canyon Trading Post has a wide variety of native art and "everyday" items such as traditional Navajo hairbrushes and weaving implements.

Opposite Top: **A summer storm builds over the Cedar Mesa sandstone hoodoos of Valley of the Gods State Park.**

Opposite Bottom: **A rock art panel overlooking the San Juan suggests this river was a travel corridor during prehistoric times.** *Right:* **The rounded tower of Hovenweep Castle stands at the head of a shallow dry canyon.** *Below:* **The villages of Hovenweep National Monument once housed a population of 2,500 or more.**

Pages 58-59: **The domed top of Navajo Mountain overlooks a Lake Powell sunrise.**

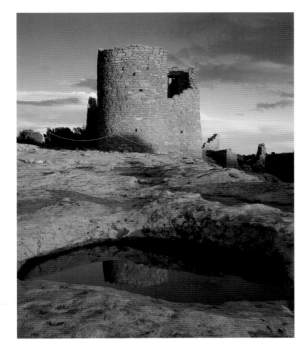

South of Bluff, Sand Island Recreation Area features ruins and rock art overlooking the San Juan River. The large number of fluteplayer images teases the imagination: Did legendary trader Kokopelli pass through here on his way through ancestral Puebloan homelands?

After crossing the Comb Ridge monocline, Hwy. 163 edges the fabulous Valley of the Gods. The scenery has inspired some to call it "Monument Valley without the crowds."

Weather permitting, you can take the seventeen-mile dirt road through reddish Cedar Mesa sandstone monoliths and buttes.

Passenger cars can also drive the forty-mile Moki Dugway, built for ore trucks carrying uranium and vanadium from Cedar Mesa to Mexican Hat. The route includes a hair-raising three miles on gravel with steep, tight turns. Or head for Goosenecks State Park, perched fifteen hundred feet above the meandering San Juan River. The curving canyon walls reveal alternating layers of Pennsylvanian-age limestone and shale deposited when this area was a hot and humid lowland.

Downriver is Mexican Hat, a prominent rock formation that looks like a man taking a siesta, his sombrero tipped forward. According to one local tale, a group of beautiful young maidens were bathing in the waters of the San Juan. Unknown to them, they were spied upon by a vaquero, or cowboy. For his boldness, he was turned to stone. The Mexican Hat locale is a popular access point for river runners hoping to ride the San Juan's famed sand waves.

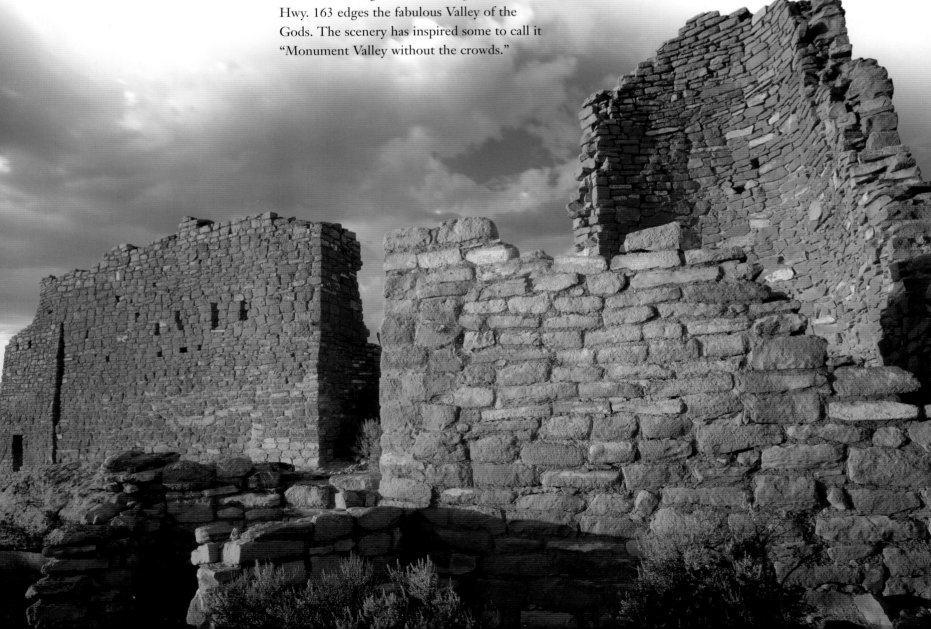

These days, river runners take out fifty four miles west at Clay Hills Crossing, where the impounded waters of Lake Powell meet the San Juan. The Navajo Reservation stretches along the lake's eastern edge, once a network of canyons leading to the Colorado River. The maze of stone between the river and Monument Valley formed a natural hideout for clans who eluded Kit Carson. Later, in 1869, John Wesley Powell's expedition floated through on their way to Grand Canyon. He named the area Glen Canyon, describing "royal arches, mossy alcoves, deep beautiful glens, and painted grottoes" and noting ruins, rock art, and ancient stairways cut into steep cliffs.

Today, much of the Glen's long human history lies underwater. In 1957 the Bureau of Reclamation decided to turn the canyon into a reservoir behind seven hundred–foot Glen Canyon Dam. It took a decade for 186-mile long Lake Powell to fill, becoming the second-largest human-made lake in the U.S., with nearly two thousand miles of shoreline, inlets, and coves that delight boaters. But big as it is, Lake Powell is only a small part of the vast Glen Canyon Recreation Area, covering 1.25 million acres of Utah and Arizona.

East of Page, the construction camp that grew into a beautiful community overlooking Lake Powell's deep blue waters, Antelope Canyon carves through the sandstone plateau. As the sun travels over this slot canyon, sculpted sandstone walls are bathed in light, shifting from deep orange to delicate lavender. It is exquisitely beautiful.

Rising above the plateau and its network of canyons is domed Navajo Mountain (Natsis'áán), where Monster Slayer and his twin returned after killing the giants plaguing the Diné. They drummed on the mountain in the first Enemy Way ceremony. Many Navajo see their land as a human figure with the mountain at its head and mesas forming torso and limbs—the embodiment of the Navajo people.

In this manner, the lands of Four Corners are imbued with the spirit of those who call it home. Their history and traditions are preserved in the landscape itself, and the drumbeats of ancient ceremonies echo in their hearts. A prayer to Navajo Mountain entreats, "Thrust out a rainbow from your brow, a rainbow from the palm of your hand—by which let me walk."

Above: Lake Powell's Gunsight Butte glows at sunset.

Four Corners Mileage Chart*

	Aztec Ruins N.M.	Bluff	Cameron	Canyon de Chelly N.M.	Chaco Culture N.H.P.	Chinle	Cortez	Farmington	Flagstaff	Four Corners	Gallup	Glen Canyon N.R.A.	Grand Canyon N.P.	Grants	Holbrook	Hovenweep N.M.	Hubbell Trading Post N.H.S.	Kayenta	Keams Canyon	Mesa Verde N.P.	Natural Bridges N.M.	Navajo N.M.	Page	Phoenix	Petrified Forest N.P.	Rainbow Bridge N.M.	Salmon Ruins	Santa Fe	Shiprock	Sunset Crater Volcano N.M.	Taos	Tuba City	Window Rock	Wupatki N.M.	Zuni
Albuquerque	178	308	340	229	134	229	274	183	333	258	137	394	411	76	232	274	191	328	271	303	365	312	394	464	236	394	170	64	231	319	132	316	162	319	175
Aztec Ruins		119	237	126	45	126	76	15	329	57	136	240	295	157	229	76	163	143	218	91	179	191	240	461	233	240	9	206	43	315	193	214	134	315	172
Blanding	142	25	196	123	177	123	83	128	259	65	189	199	253	252	243	83	158	94	177	112	52	150	199	392	247	199	140	337	100	243	364	172	165	243	225
Bluff	119		171	98	154	98	66	105	234	37	164	173	228	226	218	66	132	68	152	95	60	125	173	366	222	173	118	314	77	218	346	147	139	218	200
Cameron	237	171		175	272	175	214	223	63	184	202	82	57	265	134	214	149	97	128	243	196	47	82	196	138	82	235	401	195	47	496	25	178	47	228
Canyon de Chelly	126	98	175		161		141	112	223	92	91	166	233	153	123	141	38	69	57	170	148	148	166	355	127	166	125	290	84	206	358	152	66	206	123
Chaco Culture N.H.P.	45	154	272	161		161	121	49	353	83	118	274	329	117	212	121	153	177	253	136	253	226	274	444	216	274	37	160	77	350	165	248	125	350	155
Chinle	126	123	175		161		141	112	223	92	91	166	233	153	123	141	38	69	57	170	148	148	166	355	127	166	125	290	84	206	358	152	66	206	123
Cortez	76	66	214	141	121	141		72	331	38	137	217	272	199	230		164	120	195	29	135	168	217	462	234	217	85	282	44	316	242	191	135	316	173
Denver	362	454	625	551	407	551	379	377	778	417	583	627	682	522	678	379	636	522	606	391	465	579	627	910	682	627	371	392	405	764	287	601	608	764	621
Durango	36	109	258	158	81	158	44	50	365	83	167	260	315	192	261	44	194	163	239	56	222	212	260	493	265	260	145	211	75	347	200	234	166	347	204
Farmington	15	105	223	112	49	112	72		315	26	121	225	280	138	215	72	148	128	204	91	208	177	225	446	219	225	13	210	28	30	202	199	119	30	157
Flagstaff	329	234	63	223	364	223	331	315		231	196	145	78	257	103	331	185	161	152	359	303	110	145	155	107	145	328	395	287	16	462	88	214	16	196
Four Corners	57	37	184	92	83	92	38	27	231		119	174	229	184	216	38	133	77	180	79	157	126	174	363	220	174	72	269	31	219	261	148	120	219	158
Gallup	136	164	202	91	118	91	137	121	196	119		257	274	62	96	137	53	157	134	166	258	175	257	327	100	257	134	199	93	182	267	19	25	182	37
Glen Canyon N.R.A.	240	173	82	166	274	166	217	225	145	174	257		139	319	216	217	180	100	153	246	205	58		278	220		238	509	197	129	578	79	232	129	288
Grand Canyon N.P.	295	411	57	233	329	233	272	280	78	229	274	139		326	179	272	206	154	186	300	297	104	139	229	183	139	293	472	252	96	541	82	235	96	273
Grants	157	226	265	153	117	153	199	138	257	184	62	319	326		157	199	115	219	196	227	341	237	319	388	161	319	147	138	155	243	207	240	86	243	99
Holbrook	229	218	134	123	212	123	230	215	103	216	96	216	179	157		230	85	189	107	227	341	148	216	232	4	216	227	294	187	87	362	152	97	87	94
Hovenweep N.M.	76	66	214	141	121	141		72	331	38	137	217	272	199	230		164	120	195	29	135	168	217	462	234	217	85	282	44	316	242	191	135	316	173
Hubbell T.P., N.H.S.	163	132	149	38	153	38	164	148	185	133	53	180	206	115	85	164		104	81	192	226	122	180	317	89	180	161	252	120	11	321	126	29	11	85
Kayenta	143	68	97	69	177	69	120	128	161	77	157	100	154	219	189	120	104		95	149	143	51	100	293	193	100	141	338	100	144	406	74	132	144	189
Keams Canyon	218	152	128	57	253	57	195	204	152	180	134	153	186	196	107	195	81	95		251	273	78	153	282	112	153	229	310	178	137	379	82	87	137	143
Los Angeles	783	688	518	677	818	677	784	768	476	689	649	539	493	711	554	784	639	615	627	813	658	564	539	371	558	539	781	847	740	471	916	543	651	471	648
Las Vegas	569	475	304	463	604	463	570	554	262	450	435	271	279	497	340	570	425	374	413	599	390	351	271	286	344	271	567	633	527	257	702	329	454	257	434
Mesa Verde N.P.	91	95	243	170	136	170	29	91	359	79	166	246	300	227	227	29	192	149	251		207	197	246	490	231	246	96	296	73	345	254	219	164	345	202
Moab	194	100	270	197	233	197	115	183	334	131	248	273	328	311	317	115	232	168	251	145	174	225	273	466	321	273	196	393	156	317	397	247	239	317	284
Natural Bridges N.M.	179	60	196	148	253	148	135	208	303	157	258	205	297	341	341	135	226	143	273	207		194	205	436	345	205	221	418	180	287	459	216	233	287	311
Navajo N.M.	191	125	47	148	226	48	168	19	110	126	175	58	104	237	148	168	122	51	78	197	194		58	242	152	58	190	374	149	94	442	23	150	94	207
Page	240	173	82	166	274	166	217	225	145	174	257		139	319	216	217	180	100	153	246	205	58		278	220		238	509	197	129	578	79	232	129	288
Phoenix	461	366	196	355	444	355	462	446	155	363	327	278	229	338	232	462	317	293	282	490	436	242	278		236	278	459	525	418	149	594	221	329	149	326
Petrified Forest N.P.	233	222	138	127	216	127	234	219	107	220	100	220	183	161	4	234	89	193	112	231	345	152	220	236		220	231	298	191	91	366	156	101	91	98
Rainbow Bridge N.M.	240	173	82	166	274	166	217	225	145	174	257		139	319	216	217	180	100	153	246	205	58		278	220		238	509	197	129	578	79	232	129	288
Salmon Ruins	9	118	235	125	37	125	85	13	328	72	134	238	293	147	227	85	161	141	229	96	221	190	238	459	231	238		197	41	314	190	212	132	314	170
Salt Lake City	428	334	482	431	467	431	349	417	540	368	482	351	534	701	551	349	466	402	642	379	296	460	351	811	555	351	430	784	389	524	791	479	473	524	518
Santa Fe	206	314	401	290	160	290	282	210	395	269	199	509	472	138	294	282	252	338	310	296	418	374	509	525	298	509	197		237	379	69	377	223	379	236
Shiprock	43	77	195	84	77	84	44	28	287	31	93	197	252	155	187	44	120	100	178	73	180	149	197	418	191	197	41	237		273	231	171	91	273	129
Taos	193	346	496	358	65	358	242	202	462	261	267	578	541	207	362	242	321	406	379	254	459	442	578	594	366	578	196	69	231	449		446	292	449	305
Tuba City	214	147	25	152	248	152	191	199	88	148	179	79	82	240	152	191	126	74	82	219	216	23	79	221	156	79	212	377	171	72	446		154	72	211
Tucson	464	480	310	358	435	358	465	450	269	451	330	392	344	392	235	465	320	407	384	494	549	356	392	114	239	392	463	559	422	262	628	334	332	262	288
Window Rock	134	139	178	66	125	66	135	119	214	120	25	232	235	86	97	135	29	132	87	164	233	150	232	329	101	232	132	223	91	184	292	154		184	61
Wupatki N.M.	315	218	47	206	350	206	316	30	16	219	182	129	96	243	87	316	171	144	137	345	287	94	129	149	91	129	314	379	273		449	72	184		181
Zuni	172	200	228	123	155	123	173	157	196	158	37	288	273	99	94	173	85	189	143	202	311	207	288	326	98	288	170	236	129	181	305	211	61	181	

N.H.P. National Historic Park, N.H.S. National Historic Site, N.M. National Monument, N.P. National Park, N.R.A. National Recreation Area

*All distances are estimated.

Contact Information

Arizona Office of Tourism
1110 West Washington,
Suite 155
Phoenix, AZ 85007
(888) 520-3434
www.arizonaguide.com

Colorado Tourism Office
1625 Broadway, Suite 1700
Denver, CO 80202
(303) 892-3885
(800) 265-6723
www.colorado.com

Hopi Office of Public Information
PO Box 123
Kykotsmovi, AZ 86039
(928) 734-3283
www.hopi.nsn.us

Navajo Nation Tourism Department
PO Box 663
Window Rock, AZ 86515
(928) 871-6436
www.discovernavajo.com

New Mexico Department of Tourism
491 Old Santa Fe Trail
Santa Fe, NM 87501
(800) 545-2070
www.newmexico.org

Utah Travel Council
300 North State Street
Salt Lake City, UT 84114
(801) 538-1030
(800) 200-1160
www.utah.com

Helpful Southwestern Vocabulary

Alcove: *A shallow cave with an arched ceiling.*

Butte: *A small, block-shaped mountain.*

Cinders: *Solidified droplets of lava spray.*

Diné: *The Navajos' word for themselves; it translates as "People."*

Desert varnish: *A dark patina of manganese oxide often seen streaking cliff walls.*

Fetish: *A small stone carving, usually of an animal, carried for protection or good fortune.*

Fry bread: *Batter shaped into a circle and fried in hot fat, and the basis for a Navajo taco.*

Hogan: *A traditional Navajo dwelling, usually circular or octagonal with a doorway facing east.*

Hosteen: *A respectful title for an elder Navajo male.*

Hoodoo: *A rocky prominence eroded from soft stone.*

Kachina: *A supernatural being in Pueblo cultures. The word also refers to wood carvings that represent these beings or to the dancers who impersonate them in ceremonies. (Because the "ch" blend doesn't exist in the Hopi language, katsina is a more accurate spelling, though kachina is the most widely used.)*

Kiva: *A chamber, usually subterranean, where people gather in Puebloan villages.*

Monolith: *A tall, slender rock, also called a spire or standing rock.*

Monument: *An isolated butte or spire.*

Mesa: *Spanish word for "table," used to indicate a high, flat-topped landform.*

Prehistoric: *In the Southwest, anything predating the Spanish arrival in the 1500s.*

Pueblo: *Spanish word for "people," referring to a masonry or adobe village or the people who live there.*

Rock Art: *An image painted or drawn on (pictograph), or pecked, abraded, or incised into (petroglyph) stone. Also rock writing.*

Saddle: *A lower area between two mountain peaks.*

Sherd: *A fragment of prehistoric pottery. Also potsherd.*

Slot canyon: *A narrow, twisting, steep-sided canyon formed by repeated scouring from sediment-laden water.*

Slickrock: *Large areas of smooth rock, usually sandstone.*

Switchbacks: *Zigzagging turns in a road or trail that climb a steep grade.*

Wash: *A dry streambed that runs with water for brief periods after a rainfall.*

This page: After horses were introduced to the Southwest, the Utes hunted bison and lived in tepees, similar to these near Mexican Hat.